SJ Fowler

{Enthusiasm}

The verbal habits that they rendered fashionable are not all to be commended. By their insistence that the style of poetry should differ from that of prose they introduced the custom of employing stock poetic verbiage. They delighted in elegant variation and would use such irritating expressions as 'the feathered choir', 'the foodful brine', or 'the finny tribe'. The influence of the classics, and especially of Homer, tempted them to use compound epithets, such as 'rosy-coloured Hours', and they adopted the deplorable practice (which lasted even to the day of Keats) of adding the 'y' suffix to form adjectives and using such obnoxious words as 'plumy', 'balmy' and 'downy'. Moreover such 'poetical' words and expressions as 'verdant vales', 'solemn hour' and 'azure main' came to litter and deface their pages.

The Age of Reason Harold Nicolson

{Enthusiasm}

M.I.T.

how doth fertiliser help the bomb? / &thus
how do I intend to help thee in thy plot to
airport > to airport another airport < another
more humanity for the planes, painted pink
dip them into sudden valleys where the giant
animals have miniaturised & the miniature
here become the land where technology is not
limited by anything & the imagination of flight
is apparently a mild head cold to the viral germ
warfare we ought suddenly employ when thinking
about what we might do with our future time
the end of fox hunting, the closure of steppe
fates _ .. that golden horde of disabled will no
longer be, their limbs straightened in the womb

3

the Interrupters

> no two can meet the way we have met
> WS Graham

a foyet like the day of the dead
for it is full with missing children
this is how violence starts, first
the perception of a slight of an insult
within the context of a culture that
has taught the imperative that you must
never back down. Second, the decision
that the affront can only be answered
in a physical reprisal. So death ensues

The liver fluke cometh

though I'm dead & so very game from you
there are tugs on the seastrings running from the sea
stitched gut goggles to swim through in order you
inherit the next breathing please on in
to the next so I'm still keen as a mountain
as quick up as quiet falling off wood bars between
two quiet high points in space shuffling
rivalling the tory in the actual event, the manmade
is fielded with fat burs & begins to crank until stop
the liver fluke cometh, pack the ready bags

Though it hasn't gone very well

pity gutted in the hotel built on a wall
& though it hasn't gone very well I am afraid
if I go out my tail will freeze in pre-penicillin
wars with crows cawing in the forests
were this the past where the male version
& the not born children should elicit sympathy
sad I am to not remember that perfect line
for this poem that I had dreamed oh well
on with the end of the german basics
the lean to a spider you are afraid to become

Mercenary

famously friendship is not on a success to an insect say
so while one friend goes her way, the other shouts
assurances through the bathroom door for they
are either apart growing closer slower or it is
the inevitable decline into starting again again
I find employment in the median of We wealthiest
a sort of pale, friendless mercenary, so equipped
to deal with irascible children & a frightening
lack of perspective through example & not diatribe
there is no greater nobility at war in the borough

That really means you pay

> then holier than innocence, like ten infant commandments
> WS Graham

that really means you pay for your food
and the poverry with its brown fingerless homeless
mittens isn't so much of a freeloader through
the frosted glass, the chance to put legs on
and reload the new Irish girl with the short
call that kills an hour & I'd miss you very
much but it's an amazing idea that south
africa could be experienced as hopeful or anything
but an inconsistency & shows the possibilities
of the human mind to pretend everything is fine

The bleached is not a white

the bleached is not a white whale while I remember
it is more of a yellow, a security tag for the lion gates
as it perishes it's heart bursting in attack, the salt
water damming its arteries, the whale turns eyes down
to watch its deathplace rise into view & that's when
the mitten crabs come with their light sacks
& televisions who can sell anything and are well aware
they might mourn the recent meat but don't care
about that at all really for the on is on so
stop talking because they're watching the thing

Aboriginal prisoners of war

aboriginal prisoners of war are allowed
their Kangaroo tail delicacies even if they
have been tried by white courts and sentenced
to life and imprisoned thousands of miles from
their ancestral lands, effectively rendering
them non-homo, empty space, cleanwashed
the slave criminal turns into carriage into
such time that names are next, so impressive
to see ventriloquism of this standard, here
in the desert, where snakes have need of
their horrific poison, lest they starve

Over me climbed the brand

over me climbed the brand new clean
shaped to present the high county court judgement
the product as real living that is financial
history of women and man in order they not creep
though new towns, like Swindon, anew without
roots at least for storytelling about joy
a silent buttress on the houses of the clever
experian is the notebook of our online
personality, much more of a man than
say a fighter in the pubs and clubs of Dover

I've not the excuse of sex in a civil partnership
to release myself from the serving subletting
here I am locked, soon to be closer even

High tails for rabbits

high tails for rabbits our ready servants those
were days when nurses were quality needed
for man's device in private rooms and the happy
distance between rich and poor was as it is
then it shrunk then it grew again like
man's device which used to protein a guilt
like a water rat from a manhole, now it'd
fall past too many images of matter to mean
anything as a parasite wurm, a different
milk in denmark, an award nomination
but everyone wins the furry royal pardon vest

Setting a snare trap for a bear

setting a snare trap for a bear when a sadder
frailer trust would've been more effective
perhaps a married beam of stairs on which it
could climb, perhaps a stimulus package of
assorted meats included horse, fish and man
but not me of course, the bear being my cannibal
grandfather who swims in lye to palliate
the mentally salmon who cannot be said to
have a fine life, perhaps we should step in?

Ghosts of the civil dead

ghosts of civil dead let it not be said
that the war didn't fight in me and that I
passed war over for I was a mercenary who spread
tactics like a busy train station in which
mexican prisons were introduced to chillies
as a torture device to be hidden in the jail purse
{how I vibrated in the milk to offer a green
fruit to the central island} I cloud destiny to
leave light for madre muerte, well if the catholic
church ain't love us no more will how many
necks cut tendons cause of me with machetes

Bone can be cut

bone can be cut easy enough you just really
need to want it afterwards ask the butchers
in Spanish? the whatever like a river named
after a battle where many did die their
blood mixing with the water to the soil
like the cocktail in her veins all the
first nations of institution to the
each chip a concern with new other people
have taken to dying like buttons popping
from a shirt, an armour of fat isn't much
in the kind of fight that's coming on soon

There's the newly deaf dolphin

there's the newly deaf dolphin mothering me
again – refusing to acknowledge that it can
hear just a little but faint sounds the
moving of the {human} age upon its person
admiring a tail tethered over with music
that isn't just thinking about itself so
much that it ended up worrying about what
was on its way out and ignoring the water
everyone and their mother was swimming
in which choppy with blood but everyone
thought was cranberry juice good for the kidneys

Laid out flat upon my back

laid out flat upon my back, you cannot imagine
the feeling of my fans – the railroad worker
the others. A playground in the week the shovel
lands, drives into my human skull its not time
to plan that long a journey, its time to count
wooly animals, switch off and head for the land
of nod, where llamas await, ready to rewire a broken
jaw / wit quietens no alarm, you'd harm yourself
with your hands down, as if green curtains
were your chest, stopping you from discovering
a camp high beamed for a scale of men
who want something crowded in the plasma
of children's blood, which runs like any other
a flag on a mast and alone on the water
I feared you'd drown, & you did, in fact
pursued by the retarded child, the bean
must flee to the shell of his earth

Black eye

have you ever grappled with an eye? spinning
crutch off an irony of the damaged knee
which has no juice to protect its ball
this bed for my liver tee'd no retiree, here
today, I was lost indifferent to the guild
I let down like the leathery rope that winds
a reel of sorry / I was hungry / apologies
for I have failed lovers in broken arms
for a family but that's no excuse
manbone rusted and readied to be
prepared like a kidsaw in a cat's paw
happy hinged to lift a black eye brushed
with colour rarer and surer than the down
mind laid out with bloody coins, water
doesn't need a boat you arrogant fuck

I've been to prison

I've been to prison and patted down on the way in
this sorry event knew my being birth well blue
truffling up the treegrove I missed my pet
> my training partners > friends > family > wife >
children who in the night were snowy peaks
others ignored as locals, heaving sleds of supplies
laden with shanks, knew it I did why the back aches
as I sit before my son behind him to ask 'how
is it really inside here?'

Rice paddies

glutinous rice paddies with hot leaves
with sauce, men buried up to their necks
and the dead ones up to their foreheads
returning to vietnam to exhume the bodies
that was the war and not the museum
of doubt / death / debt where I do my work
exchanging money for time and where doing
endless circles I found my wife, waving
for the first two years and talking for the rest

My nose is bleeding

> In him the blood with arm an iron monk
> WS Graham

My nose is bleeding, its close quarter combat
CPC with a black seagull, I must be a kiddie
again Newquay being kissed on the bacon fields
all those pigs, it must definitely be a dream
with the driving the fond event into a tree
we were promised more space in this room
are you okay with each other now? yes
after the knockout we become great friends
never sleep on a giant, something like
the ingredients of sorcery

raw potatoes are better than nothing
its all I can endure to pass, the death of
not having is not imaginable in my nature
no more real than a 10th collection
mock execution, thirst, I'd better prepare

Endure no comets

how do you pleasure and approach the prize?
WS Graham

endure no comets, put into word no apoc
alypse its just not worth the hassle and
not accurate measure of guilt on hill
with your 'family' having left the safety
of your food stocked bunker behind
you are willing to face armageddon
face first liking the firing squad – you are
human stronghold, a lost eye jelly made
of stemcells scared of future sermons
in which you aren't around to see it all
flush away like the giant long weeded
and silver that it frankly is

You can't hear nothing

you can't hear nothing but your own regret
in gardens, at times, mystifying that you
left the city behind because it turns out
you can't sleep here either, and the people
but at least the potential pet ownership
fell down a well and found a bone, that must
mean it happened for a reason for now we
have a bone to throw but for the restriction
the backpack enforces like a sat beetle sat
calmly knowing it won't be able to up

No limit to the resources

no limit to the resources I can draw together
to make my neman arch mausoleum ossuary
the bird fly put paid to economy and now
burning torches sit comforted atop pyramids
of the human skull which are so full of
pethadide to be terrorism for a near goblet
warming us to hide, and don't drink, it's not
in no way good for you, pill instead, stop the
spread of regrettable architecture, use bone

Further nosebleeds

> I am a parliament in a roaring way
> WS Graham

facilitating nosebleeds the old fashioned way
with a whip backfist, a turning side
a plantation operation for the not black nearly
happy as man breaks / gov't to be nearly free
love to vote on the raw red ribbon of the gang
that only a vigilante justice can bring to its
knees to drink itself together tilting order
of spirit to keep populations ~ a new hat
for pain, gloves for a quiet war, a warm break
for the bone of pleasure that is civil social work

Sansho the bailiff

portrait is in the nature of a self-confession
on first plane to hungary, auditioning in szerz
with michelle wilde, what are / is she doing with her life?
managing an estate agent's, collecting money from
some insignificant toy farm, 18, not allowing her
to decide the spam runs out brown
onto my belly, this is Ogai defending Japan
to the German press, this is a make her eat it up politely
& she doesn't mind because I find Kelly
I'm glad she doesn't like it that & keep doing so
open to get at apart, I shouldn't have sparked her drink
with fibre but she cries with embargo
for 13 years famine has been a game to all of you
but now what you will do will only make it worst

Great scandal catches

if the cold meze is cold food what shall
we do while we wait? cry about it – under
it, well if we can afford a house in Holland
park I'm not sure I have a right to reminisce
in horror at what James described as slave
punishment, when Hector was forced to shit
in the other one's mouth, after all those who
remained celebrated, long after the fact
would it happened so often, and is so essential
to woman + man it's impossible to begin
at making sense of it. To which I'll say I
imagine every single incident of disembowelling
in a row, born again, born again, up with
the swamp water comes a myst & a music

Quidistant in 4 parts

punishment trek to find the latest innocent
a way to market food to human minds that do
not possess hungry bodies up the up in
the hills with their distilleries brewing
out the clean + the clear because they're bored
well come finally to more of me & then that'll
fall aside because I won't be able to get to sleep
in the meantime it's tempting to copy + paste
the lyrics of Peter Gabriel + Kate Bush
don't give up cause you need that   flower
blood on the most modern phones travel
at an angle up, / child preaching childhood
sleep introduced to interruption, the black
bags before the eyes of children, later
weeks – the strain on Peter for he is great
the Great, dancing, hammer amidst the spray
the demented shine used to get that monsters
metal car so heavy solid looking new
weighing more than a polar bear
bluegrass to the very floor, I'm sorry you weren't
better welcomed but after all our jobs took you

Cartels

you dropped your in the gutter? all those
you never read & out there those cartels
chewing endlessly cutting off peoples
heads for their mother & their fingers for
their police you're right those mementoes
thoughts before the knife hits neck ...
whether I'm interested is a leader or not
but you can go home as far as I'm concerned
if I want to mention people you haven't
read, well that's your problem

Balmy

for the eclectic whip cracks children light
prostitute of the 80, lipstick, dressing gown
throats & event horizon, someone, burst in space
a film at the end of the street how one cut
the funeral for that friend who wouldn't go
is gone into the already known
the crust on its uppers, a bow on a box in west
acton is a human being learning to live in our world
paddington; the feet hardly moving
the fingers twitching to check our phone
I'm only just onto Paul Blackburn but I will
stay on him / I'm glad the venus nebula
is ever expanding because I'll not stop following
its expansion / there's always new & the catalogue
next to me can fuck off online where
man ray imagined women's mother milk well
well enough / love / hands between the feta crouch
for the 2 fingers in the greek pie / hard roast meat
I hope to be well dead before you run out gassing
in the oven to invert those appreciating those working
who worked before the gas but now a shame
why did I watch the 4th Underworld film?
hot food, for hot food

Burn museum

the gypsy wound
fighting man of a fighting family
bitterly pain full is a broken jaw, a bruised
kidney
it'll make you think twice, modern Paul
it doesn't just hurt, it's worse
it drifts its bookish suitcase
like a river of shirt toward work
a life of petty retreat, no more square
nose biting, not a real drift
& not too fair to go with them people
there are not enough to extinguish
to reflect how much hate there is
everywhere in every corner of living
a tomb of trinkets, a shackle
to the meaningless corrupt interpretation
of the recent past

Bath with Marlborough

If a baby dies in Bristol does it not rot
attracting maggots it does so why am I not
allowed to kill now before I've gone
in newcastle? standing outside the strip
deals working as a day, a door I see
4 bags + 1 bag & them a bottle go into
the boys face & run down + punch
the knifing boy in the ear, which rips
from the force of my punch but to him
the stabbed boy has been stabbed
in the linguistically & not the mock & he's
closing mam mam please help not to stall
me about jesus helping me mum my chest
burning grind me you don't know jesus
he can't pull the knife out but I am
& pull out the knife which is timing
& I later learn is a mistake & I got arrested
as the ear boy is 15 & I never work the door
again luck to not set a conviction

Lore

the heat of everyone is corrupt
if you expect more than that
otherwise, there exists no one
organised enough to maintain conspiracies
of inhuman enough to keep secrets
bear in mind that if you do expect
more than transfer like a base to base inheritance
you will be shocked to far more than you
could've imagined in the hearts of everyone
for my partner I believe I am redeemed by how
thinly veiled my dog is on the fellows
the highstreet going
there are other things too, things I do with my hands

Cured meat

a baby is cruel
as a crystal baby {ball}
in its eye you can't see
romania
+ that is the fault
of the crystal pipe
which replaces everything alive + ruined
with a red dart cabbage
which was once Crystal baby
you cannot replace it, break it, ruin it
it dies to protect
perfect insulation material

Hard hunter

muslim baby is a hard hunter
of the wicked, wiping sweat
seems a profession parents are proud of
walky talky: on
book ontop of a wardrobe
everyone needs to find true love
the bloom is not a flower
it's a scar, glowing bees
don't leave the baby by the shoes
outside the mosque mate

Bed eater

baby eats the bed
late for a meeting
rusk is made of soaring horse
no paperwork for the supply chain
bare chest summer baby isbraun
pickled tin has the same name
no limits to its weekend
the car in the murder cloud, the lake
the baby has only one colour
milk of the poppy tit

god himself was a baby

god himself was a baby lady
creating comedy, mills – ladybirds
refried beans – there were no limits
to the Seventh day rest
braided baby beard
white as a polar bear
I knew him then, before he had changed
before social serves let him down

<u>when do we ask Why</u>

when do we ask Why the parents
hated their baby? it's got so
maybe it was a provocateur
disarming the boiler, leaving the gas
on – maybe it wouldn't go on to say story
maybe talentless, hungry
shattered after a day it gave up
disappointed their expectations
more cheeks fired would save babies
I think – breed breed in the meantime
names of my tongue
beads scroched in prawn

Cub

a bear I am I am with rubber claws
cradling a swaddled china baby
the infant whose family crest
is a mad pipe – not a swinging pipe
not a bolo baton
but a made-in-chelsea china concrete cigar
which was the 59th of its name
Cristy's clit & it's not scary
when you've seen quite a few of them

Social services

theroots of social services is in the throats
of socialist labour, when they were Left, which
began with Jesus Christ who was a Jewish
lady who giggled when lifted and whose
breasts jiggled when he was shook
which was a little bit out of order
+ where were his guardians then? where
were the social services? endemic failures
across the board as standards + morals are not
changed from 2013 years ago in the middle eastern desert

Mutu

baby mutu drove a minivan into a wall
of nipples and came out sucking his thumb
covered in the airbag's powdered milk +
later on, after Chelsea, he couldn't even
finish his breakfast because of that
Baby 59 + his suffering, who was obviously
sent by god for adult mutu, + whose pain
was worse than all those ununnumbered
romanian babies who'll have to get in
line tv ultra reports adult mutu's wife
said ok and now there's a coke party in
ajaccio to celebrate the adoption though
romania is not listed on china's baby exile list

the baby of the north

the baby of the north is more likely
to be an alcoholic, unemployed + eating the
fatty foods like chops but has a funny
accent rather I'd be running back to my
wife a norse salesman selling skald
don't let a baby wear what it wants
it is a baby that is your choice leaving
difficulties, don't feed a dog dark chocolate
it'll die, Lance Armstrong raised so much money
for cancer research that his cheating is
irrelevant you + if I see you outside
a supermarket smoking at your toddler
I will sink my thumbs into your jugular

virgin mary

the virgin mary might not have been
fucked but she didn't have a caesarian
so all the more stretching horror cuts
when baby J meloned out – a conception
like chess where man + woman can play
without it ending up regrettable – can
you imagine what it would be like
if Erika, Aurelie or Hitzeman got pregnant?
not good news, not good + abortion

Karate

master bear made me, says the talking
baby to the silent parrot, but then he
left me, he had, ask to do in Porto,
then Oviedo, Virginia commissioned him to
paint the royal family in words and choosing
between money + life he made his choice.
when I am a grown up sexy girl I'll get
my revenge – I'll key his fancy car

Black eagle

in 1200 the english longbaby made chain
mail redundant, it went right fucking
through, then armour, of course, you understand
but then there were guns, after gunpowder
thanks China, then in 1970 the english
invented mailart + just 13 years later
I was fucking born and then allergies
were all over and roasts on bloody sunday
what is the cost of living honourably?
much much more than you would think

Shunga

baby my lesson is that the entity of
knowledge is a big fat tear
this is the safest time to have ever been
alive + men have always had murders
+ mistresses, I'm not that sorry, others
aside from their family for going
because the male libido is genetically
programmed to procreate as much as
is possible + that isn't my fault because
it was invented back in History by monkeys
or your god of your choice if you like
to be an idiot

Immersion heater

baby in the bath my inheritance to you
is hundreds of half brothers + sisters, each
one a different shade of pinkish brown
depending on their assorted mother's race
be nice to each other, you share blood +
remember an american accent almost always
sounds thick + I'll bury the treasure you'll
need to buy your robot citizenship when
they take over by the old fucking tree

Out for justice

baby bullet you're legal in somewheres
and knives too if only one side is edged
I feel safer already, and am suddenly legally
prepared to cut your umbilical cord
in africa they eat placenta, in Spain eggcake,
in Greece pie, but we aren't there we're here
so babymush + some tempura wearing a wig
will be absolutely 100% fine thanks for asking

Nico

cot death is caused by god's wrath + bad parenting
is cot death the disease where the child
grows up to be a duck? if not I retract
the first line of the poem, if so I will instruct
my baby in the filipino martial arts so
that its skill will be such that it can
destroy the endless barrage of idiots that it
will encounter – a true threat we really don't
want to test it

Retrospective when the artist is still alive

baby bowie one eye green one blue
you sing Berlin down. I like that but I don't
believe my friend Alex that often so I
prefer Alice Eve though she's posh whose
body you saw in starek into dkarness
which also launched beneland cumberbatch
not one of them are a match for the protection
afforded by the best quality deodorants
an offer though smelly girls pits are awestruck

Valhalla

bloody stumps, imagine the battles! how
unreachable, so much like beautiful
girls who were babies whose fathers had to
let go, to find inspiration elsewhere
beauty is beauty no one matters where from
it comes, its there to be nosed, she runs
where she once crawled, I swing a plastic
mace on a freshly minted whitewashed wall
to crush daddy long legs where I once would
ve utterly destroyed a human skull with an axe
+ celebrated for it, things have changed so
I've done alright considered the size of the transition

Night shift

there are late nights...then there are late night things
welcome to turkey and its beach and its pretty
+ remember to bring toilet paper with you
hope I didn't get you in trouble baby, with my fang!
step twice back, ache not as much as you thought
& understand you stroke gold with asturias, in spain
understand the crispy one, just the french duck
that leave us speakless – a baby being made in the oven
let's pretend this never happened

That hurt my ears

I have practised removing it from my pocket
mine games so covered but questioned use of music
I watched you receive your shape
the ice is broken & he's close to death, there
some people shine, some dull
human cities, & today we playfully woke up to
a shoal of baby Orcas playing in the sunshine it
harms
people >>> grinder = payback has a new name
everyone's a critic. it's a good idea, but it doesn't work so well
to rob the dead & help the living

Butter

for Glyn F.

Tell me they tell me I aren't brave
& confused   I get   up
burnt with a solid shame
better my brother says
to have been able to let fighting go
war he means
my friends in Afghanistan
butter my brother says
is very tatty

Speciality of the throat

if these painters represent our time then we are going mad
nick-e melville says after listening to arabic
"I didnae understand any oe that" & the impressive
woman from Kurdistan says she's descended
from sunflowers which is a bath of balls
in the mean Kyle Dake won his 4th national
in his 4th weight class & we're hot speaking
of mental strength
what would writings know of that
they did very little to close the book on aids
very little to scare those russian advisors
who would advice you !"don't carry too much uniform"
& don't cook all night, it starves
how different the world might have been
if he had gone on his golfing tour to Scotland
consider the legion, gaming, consider acting
why crush the republic? there is more here
than talks about talks
something is wrong with the world
       & these men know

Letters to friends

lovers in the concrete
village
setting in the wet
Wishes
to peacefully
cover graciously
the Problem
love to you
sincerely
out info
rmation
you weeping
yellow eyes
nighttime snack keeps me fat
body shaking
death throes
is not a dance

the exhausted mesaba of their dangling breasts
soft wax structures to support our collectively ceaseless greed
Ed Dorn

as ephemeral as it is a colon is not a delusion
& that black > Meatgrinder > sausage.
is not actually talking but speaking so impressive
I'm not an academic said at a conference
if you say it to my face I'll end up again
the intersection of ear & teeth the molestation
of a reality you really have no clue about
a standard of living that precludes, his song
a providence / birthday / spear in the citizens
you are the housewife / I'm used to the drink

We deserve better for the money

we deserve a better garden for the money
a mare ridden into a warm, closed street
where its free days are sleepcare
alcohol is not present here
has not a smudge of presence ever
allow this imparting – never regretted that
day of the dead parade sober
else we'll fall asleep with the standard
& drop it on the hospital steps

<u>An arrogance that appears as though</u>
<u>they forget humans are equal when</u>

blowdryer that performs piano
& the seaside worth noting, the baltic beach
I used to be scared of the Whales bow
now I make the best of the little light
afforded me in the Museum
cool building with which to work with
show me please the fine paper
keeping figure hush at the crib
it's glow played time, incidental hand touching
my grip on your ribs, teaching proper breathing
& a defensive stance for features heavy
opposite of avoiding – seeking
it lies down to sleep, that's it
a pleasant night, nowt died

Healing as a planet

saw to Ealing as a planet earth
going to its slow growth
a place begging vegetable
sombre, health seeking, much a taste acquired
in time, application & practice
for health in wisdom
big ball of blue veined envy & ambition
missing the high st. when on holidays
you have a home, sad lurch of our suburb
red road bezerker full of family

Nicholas of Healing

Urdu draughtsman in Polish paints perfect
a still life mirror which reflects a further life stare
that just gets up & gets on with it everyday
End of Watch, Alps & Argonauts
true few ways around that kind of heart
is the sturdy a tapir? or a Tetris elephant?
I'd rather be Lenkiewicz than a bank manager
change / or die
the river as a friendly story of a disaster
black green pine trees
forever going to live in Ealing because of money

for Oscar S.

in the preface to armed conflict there is
centred sat a man, writing, & he who
went out there a teacher is now collecting
information for 'the security industry' with
their offices in bloomsbury, appreciation
is ours of the warmode checked by our
own pride, that we really believed
that we had 'fixed' the language of it
eternally & had reached the perfection
which dominates a classical age – they
sit around transvaal ranches with shitty
pensions & wait for the next year. ~~they who'd~~
redwater bluewater blackwater Sandlines
military force not aligned to a nation or gov't
is a force for good (when they work Pro Bono)
& I say this on the day NK says they'll
launch their New Clears tomorrow which
is a worrying box headline to read on yahoo news
no more emails after that ... no matter what matter
can exist where the people – no matter how small
I don't have to explain myself to you in
the form of a source of New Information
he has a black glass eye, on the 4th day
the butt of an Angolan rifle smashed the
natural eye from his head & he says this
without ~~a concern~~ drama

Buffalo love

ample Hello annoying child
I have your ample Hips
now shut up, I am not patient
money, not a river / A lot more
girls smile at me since I became
older
in the last white sun that arrives
I stare at her end, her lips part
very little snow + peasantry
vagrant talk of greek crises
small islands attached to other lands

Cathedral Voyage

us if to disgust the bourgeois parrental
heel of my private school girlfriend
what oer her arse when we were 16 & he couldn't
walk properly the following day & told her friends
& I did it to one of them too, wiping my hand
over their elicits horsepower colonies, money
from a kind racetrack incursion arms manufacture
black horses in six dripping with port black hats
of steaks a big blue bon child with all fork
hungry for more no one has bledenough
seemed my war is quietly endless

Murmansk

it was I that began to cease learning when the coffin lid closes
the russians had an inordinate affection for coffins
sometimes having them laid out waiting for months, even years
before death, to rather eat a cask of shit than return to russia
the only defence is head down / hands up
to say we didn't do it   because we couldn't have done it
a filial son would in good conscience
purchase his parents' coffin long before it was thought to be needed
and the elders would even take to sleeping in them in preparation.
It was thus believed an act of great merit – so great as to offset evil deeds
– to purchase coffins for the poor who could not afford their own.

> sometimes there was an arm or leg
> leftover,
> it lay around until the next shipment;
> they made it fit in somewhere
> > Gerald McCarthy

should I begin as if it were a story for in (not during wartime)
they mistook a story for a poem as often as
I'm not saying you never had it so good
but that is a fact, isn't it? we had the touch & feel
I cannot tell you what to do but I can show you
if everywhere you put your thumb on the soil there is a plant growing
then we have a chance to be happy
the French union, is it a circle?
or is it a square?, earth is a square
heaven is a circle, a night hunting rats with only our wits
how long would you like to fight? you pick the term
for we are not under bombing we are facing it
what is feared is a story that explains itself
so much it almost isn't there upon its end
the helicopter gun that's known as birth control

the City

always be a beloved space of trans. to accept what is
greed in pets not so much in reasons
for the closed will open in matters of delicate urgency
for a winter bonus to clam his prescience
because bark numbers anyway
suicide was induced by / with octopus limbs & no teeth
gorging on the tesco finest
departed in the city night to let their actual well
where weeping & smiling fits of those still asleep
comes in place beside you not gambling
poor eye bandaged & lead them stumbling to the sea
where they can repopulate the oceans
may their mouths never shut, gasping for water
for if you were ever hungry, would you dream
of how you are to slice the meat? or whether
you would hold a fork, or a spoon? or neither?
or the angle the food would enter your mouth?
so why is it so when what he calls mating
mixed with paper? this is money he imagines
eating

Hands harp

In nothingness questions dwell
Ernst Meister

thank the thought
of thinking
thank the night
of drinking
Kaspar's still dead
the grand piano
in his stead
is missing strings

Exercise

I dream   lions growing on the savannah
Jèssica Pujol I Duran

I smashed my hand by dropping my squat
weight on the same day I pushed an older
man over near holborn. A strange day of close
shaves, with some disturbed feelings of guilt
or worry at the risk of those moments, she
couldnt have been more caring, it continues
to a perfect time between us, so much good
feeling for a month. We talk a lot too, it has
never been easier to be with someone.

the smaller death drive today, a near tendency
toward experiencing the exhaustion of some
thing, though false and shallow, that is like dying
transference of hatred, unable to assault those
who wish to pour this vitality that would be self
defeating into a victimless act of catharsis
humours, just the act of interruption to disrobe
during the day, to wear what inevitably
were more comfortable clothes, to shower

game of thrones is becoming a pursuit of thought
not sure what that measures. I am open to whatever
our trip to dungeness was beautiful, we should
buy a house collectively. I lost my temper, I cannot
bear her that way, defiant. I don't linger on this
none the less, I shouldn't have grabbed her
wrists. End of g.o.t. was amazing, dragons,
surprising deaths. Been a good week since the
slip, to see the lambs, three lovely nights together.

Straw

in my region, we say thank you
René Char

a range of the great music misled
turns into weapons, turn into your bed
touch the tips of your unloved
and intend to drive the other's into death
I have not betrayed my own
I have not killed a day so small
it is almost a canal
stray, chip of the lives

Our cousins from Abroad

& were it not for my glasses I'd not be reading, a new
in love with a lecturer, a stereotype event in 1923 even
a lot of first wives are fascist & its hard to think what he might
say if he were to speak out in plaid, a tunic, forest tweed
talking to the birds while the doctor is busy with his green
gorilla & his black dolphin a touring Circus
with Wolfgang & his daring Lottie
yet I have no interest in preserving the job
whilst retreating & biding time to see
on the water who will win, I hope its the darling
kind of thinking, if being a peasant
is so good ... why toenails pile up like rubber tires
while a blind meal for the men with the most sight
so makes trouble for drowning
in a backwoods retirement community
fashion, turns out she is more physically attractive
than Hannah so while organ banks are full
our prepared skin is a visit
she carries our brother's child, alarmed
as if to rush to board a train

the spectre of miniature women
the journey ruined, in my bag, her hairclip, and socks
and the books she was worrying about
indeed she doesn't come off well
waiting for me to arrive and at home, at dinner;
I take to the woods with Martin
where the pulpits are full with pinecones
a portrait of Pascal and a signature HH
avoid eating with their conversation and its consequents
the root is interspersed with sculptured cabins
they are the tunnels throughout the land, running beneath gates
with hatches that can't be seen within his burrow
I remember the peeling of a lamb & our first meal of meat
& the knitting of the bones, I thought, she is partly right
we touched, fingers to breasts, perhaps,

in retrospect, against her will
though soon she was combing her hair
'if you guarantee me a living you can have these in return'
like closing a lid I shut my mouth, & in the later writings
who is it that is qualified? the relentless not certificated?

the water, the net   a nightmare about a millipede
with pistons, blinking, feeding off patients
suppressing lost light again
paralysing the pause, the physic anorex seeping
greeting beneath covers as the unnoticed growth
of a paunch as though boredom sits quiet beneath our coats
successful but wanting to be alert, ears up,
he skins over the flesh that collects around the breast
incising the breastbone and running down to the anus
he listens to the whisper; this means the lungs have emptied.
keep the leg bones attached to the toes
the toes keep attached to the hip, secure the spine
keep the flesh in the paws, leave the wings
use no chemicals, it is in the posing, the hiding, that
the bird offers herself to us most truly
mounted on his wall, the fourfold, the worlds behind
flapping about

How hopeful, how hopeful is the landscape
of Southern Spanish Speakers

though we are barely friends we holidayed
together & when you left the room to shower I
milled, I grasped her throat, & led the witness, &
threatened her should she tell you of what I
was to do to the pajamas you left on the bed
I sniffed the crotch they were not yet dry
the other girl soiled her underwear through fear
having witnessed what I warned her she would
have witnessed & not be allowed to speak of
which led to more difficulties when I had to tear
them from her & smell them & then prise
open her legs which is how you found us when
you came back into the room from the bathroom
& got the wrong impression because the only
reason I went on holiday was that you would
come with me & that I might get a chance at
your used clothes & we might live together

73

Noisey machine lack

the shared joke
how to become a saint through suffering
the stairs we cannot afford
the smells
burnt hair, the rusted perch
in the cellar of a church
reenactment is moving but not accurate
as though an alarm would sound for work
like white noise, A are quiet
the figure descends
in premonition of the home of the martyr
a holiday, again,
a radio is searching for a station
the damage done all in a brief visit

the doctor stands by
fondling the crevasse

Nattvardsgästerna

the superhighway is naturally the pillars cement
lined with jagged
contribution
in the abandoned mineshaft being built to cross the north sea. It will begin
at the mouth of örnsköldsvik, the pitch is car-
cass. The tarmac itself is ground with black sand and turquoise shale
children wade. Just a man's coral. It is not escapable.
up bone and tooth. Gustav's length out
us, and in turn
the water. The taste will not be known a sheep floats, up turned winking
                                        at the sun
to sea there is a sheerface drop
Harold. The underwater cliffledge there
on Gunnar's farm there is a well more to their despair that fresh water
is available freely, for granted they will take   sits a spike, Tomas
though the hole is perrilous and black unseen from the woods
for thickly bound branches are laid on as a lid. It is a trap

a beach, visited just one season of four

75

Russian bear

she is washing her niece's bear under the glare of her auntie
her niece   is all but eight months old, and all
that wasted soap, but she too is convinced
when the bear smells like
                                              flour
shame   the bear is a government list
writing common sense articles for a liberal russian newspaper
    soon to disappear Ekaterina = FSB, shot in stairwell
torture – OD30 dual text columns (line of questioning)
& in what profession
excitedly I see myself controlling mother
mensmotion with a bayonet
& extracting information through a wet towel
pliers / electrically "the pond is full of birds
& glass"   Protection for the Viscera

Improvised immortal

not concentrating is drying the sweat
around the brow of the dappled
turns out there are Caligula
covered bonds nesting, getting a metallic
wish   not remaining silent
really not to talk to tinsel rings
a dusty facade, the glare blinds
not listening to mobile signals
no lofty fingers strangers
foremost rehabilitation on the roadside

and;

to place carefully into a black rubber bag

Boys on prague film

he likes
for bus station)
draped in a back his side and his fists clenched
his left leg is the heightened in a, nude by advanced
(ancient karian on a bier east greek strictly frontal stance
his arms of potential movement could be mutual
though it would be intentional his ears with wax,
and at his request. loincloth. represented
hired
sighing, plugs impression apis bull lying the kouros type,
from boiotia eerie he has no
is tied to the mast. already on the register

of obscure public speakers I set the purpose of his poetry
is sligh lecture series totally forgotten, how do you know who is
I have support act those hanging to denounce my control
overbearing, they say, 'even a man who can't pretend
remembrances, miming when a travelling circus to be
   quarter naked   icing trailing a line remembering
what & when? I say the whole of Gateshead might be thinking
of him   this very minute   he was one of those
is a them their topics they have met in private
  though I too doubt that   they are dancing alone
before their laptop computer   chin to the their groins
      so quiet   make them recite   the forgotten, who dwarf

The last few days of civilian life for Israeli girls

when the flooded die fighting began it was wet loosed
making an I speak for the appeal to admission only man
in the room with skin, see it before you
I hope of war in decades   coloured & burning hair
how it is before tampering, grows used to
the young animals, my prostration   at gunpoint
    & a smell one
women
          about to begin their duties
i am the   the problem
    toned   core
     to love another
     concrete   talking

They will have dried by December

En Coeur en hiver best described true, it just ages
ends it arbitrarily = Turkey as a bird that took to smacking
its beak like the world was a war, as though pornography
cocaine isn't also eastern, there, like an apple is eaten
so some seeds force you to stop / do it, somewhere, also
talk around in the dark, re-greetable, though if we hadn't
been on our own it could've been so much better
a series ... athletes with water cannons warm around
our necks as we close in on deforestation in Istanbul
the high st. our friends poisoned, it's white beauty
of yet again ... police versus army, people versus the
hidden elites, with their own private beauty? rest
assured, if something lands we will pick it up
your enemi, temporary, time relativity, transitory
territory "I'm afraid when anyone says for you I will
lay down my life"   that stretches beyond that river lamb
a caused way square, grown three dimensional
to contain people, because it is boxed at birth
its meat = a cake half, I could find water, it'd become
water, the rains of Castemere, a play, o now there's
water, tied up in this, a concern, embrace the grind
embrace the selfish, the 'what do you care about?'
the lamb squeaks, pain is just weakness leaving a body
beyond the country   but we are with the crowd not the country

There's a lot worse people than me walking about

They will have died by December

The rivers of Turkey, I say
Özdemir İnce

an island it is the river flapping arms rising
the league of flowers if Turk for nothing specimen of waste
a purple headband dreams of sushi
river lines. Tatar. tamerline eats babies.
my morbid 8 year old wants to see dead bodies
made of water, stabbed long before the Bosphorus
                        give back waterlogged bodies
up to Galata hacking and drown, choking it is
to like a seabirdbody full of the river underwater
flows into nose unlike any other river except the mouth
like stilettos upon and clasping a handbag
plump with liquid, and gazes by wallow
the land fires, so long, as wide as the river
the soil in the water more on a bellyful float

Plumy

English league of defenders you were that clever
from the beginning of the rest of the world
a dementia thru diet, what have we really
learned from the nearly dead not dead
... plenty of like ghost voices from those pits
where not a sun gets in, still the drugged pint
their villages, they're pretty violent places
I've been the stained land burned as it didn't
make it secret ivory for the willing to work
but can't get it at it blind to I'm writing too much
in the morass into every no one reads internet
magazines but away I go, slug trails
maybe that proves I'm doing it right
the Icelandic oriental stokes an ice pipe
musicians are replaced, their throats slit
guitar strummed golden embroidered with
monkeys + foxes the walls painted yellow
the colour of disfavour
I erupt from a long line of brilliant administrators
owning the world that way
are there places still more beautiful than that?

Irrationality as a gender

We too believe in your hands tied up
the field of lambs is sturdy, propped
on concrete pillars as the other earth
I promise we will eat while we watch
it return to the rotten molten core
& maybe meet there? early next year?
golden deer makes for tasty steak
& like us I feel terrible guilt that I
shot it, but I just won't tell anyone
which is a rarely achieved human feat
& is highly unlikely, for, of course, the
ghost of the deer will always know
my tribe hates love & "I'm going to stop
pretending I didn't break & was
just that clear good. I love you too, winch
I love sleeping softly, the creak of the
swinging bill, the rustling of purse notes
so I can restock my ball bearing armoury
books are clear on it, the will fall blinded

{Enthusiasm} by SJ Fowler

Published by Test Centre in 2015 in an edition of 400 copies
of which 25 are signed, numbered, and contain additional
holograph material.

Text copyright © SJ Fowler
Designed by Traven T. Croves
Printed by ArtQuarters Press
www.testcentre.org.uk

Front and back cover images from Wellcome Images.
Front: Line engraving, c. 1780. Wellcome Library, London,
           no. 562080i. Photo no. V0008019EL. Human skull
           with chin tilted downward.
Back: Line engraving, c.1780. Wellcome Library, London,
           no. 562084i, Photo no. V0008020ER. Human skull,
           seen from above.

ISBN: 978-0-9926858-6-7